The Journey of Motherhood
Strength, Love & Resilience

"Behind every strong child is a mother who learned to rise above her own storms."

Vgdawson

Books on Friendship, Relationships, and Personal Growth

Books on Personal Growth and Life Reflection

Unlocking Your Best Self

Setting Boundaries with Family & Friends

Books on Relationships and Personal Boundaries

My Best Friend

The Friendship Years

Books for Readers Life After 50

The Truth about the Golden Years: What Aging Really Reveals

Discover More

Visit the author online for additional books, resources, and inspiration:

www.what2buynext.com

THE JOURNEY OF MOTHERHOOD
Strength, Love & Resilience
Copyright © 2026 by VaNessa G. Dawson

Published by
Second Season Press
Birmingham, Alabama
www.what2buynext.com
ISBN: 978-1-972518-12-0

Cataloging information is available from the Library of Congress.
Library of Congress Control Number: 2026912796
First Edition: 2026

Printed in the United States of America

The author and publisher do not guarantee any specific outcomes. Every mother's journey is unique, and results may vary.

To every mother who has ever questioned her worth, doubted her strength, or felt alone in the journey; this book is for you.

To the women who became mothers young, later in life, by choice, or by surprise; you are powerful, resilient, and enough.

To the single mothers navigating parenthood from day one without the steady presence of a partner, I see you, I honor you, and I wrote these words with you in mind.

And most intimately...

To my daughters-in-law,

I know the road hasn't been easy. From the moment your children were born, you carried the full weight of parenthood on your own shoulders.

Not all men are cut out to be husbands or fathers, and that truth, while painful, does not define your worth.

You are showing up every single day with courage, love, and strength. You are raising strong, beautiful children despite the odds, and that is no small feat.

This book is a tribute to your quiet sacrifices, your loud victories, and everything in between. You are doing the work of two with the heart of one, and for that, I admire you deeply.

With all my love and respect,

Vgdawson

Table of Contents

Motherhood is one of the most profound journeys a woman can experience. It is a role filled with love, sacrifice, resilience, and an unwavering commitment to shaping the lives of the next generation.

Yet, the path of motherhood is not the same for everyone. Some become mothers at an early age, facing unexpected challenges. Others wait until later in life, embracing the experience with wisdom and patience.

Some do it alone, while others navigate the partnership of co-parenting. And then there are the women whose children never fully leave, creating a new dynamic in the ever-evolving role of motherhood.

This book explores the different stages and experiences of motherhood; the joys, the struggles, the lessons, and the moments of pure gratitude. It is a tribute to the resilience, empowerment, and courage that define every mother's journey.

Through personal reflections, shared experiences, and heartfelt wisdom, my hope is that you find comfort in knowing you are not alone. Motherhood is not about perfection; it is about love, endurance, and the ability to keep going even when the road is uncertain.

No matter where you are in your journey, this book is a reminder to embrace your role, celebrate your victories, and find strength in the challenges. Because at the heart of it all, motherhood is a beautiful, complex, and rewarding experience that deserves to be honored.

Motherhood is not a singular experience. It is a journey that unfolds in countless ways, shaped by circumstances, choices, and sometimes fate. While society often places motherhood within a rigid timeline or expectation, the reality is that no two mothers experience the path the same way.

Some enter motherhood unexpectedly in their teenage years, others wait until later in life, and many face challenges on the road to becoming a mother, whether through fertility treatments, adoption, or unconventional means.

This chapter explores the different ways women become mothers, the struggles and triumphs along the way, and the lessons that shape them into the resilient, nurturing, and powerful women they become.

Teenage Motherhood – Challenges and Triumphs

Becoming a mother as a teenager is not the path most envision for themselves. It is a journey often met with judgment, challenges, and obstacles that seem insurmountable.

However, teenage mothers are among the most resilient women, finding strength in unexpected places and proving that love knows no age.

The Unexpected Reality

For many teenage mothers, the moment they see a positive pregnancy test is life-altering. In an instant, their world shifts from the carefree days of adolescence to the heavy responsibilities of parenthood. Some face fear and uncertainty, worried about how their families, friends, and society will react.

Others are met with love and support but still struggle with the emotional and physical demands of pregnancy at a young age.

School, friendships, and future aspirations often take a backseat to prenatal visits, morning sickness, and preparing for a baby.

There are moments of doubt—"Am I ready for this?" "Can I be a good mother?" "How will I manage?"—but there are also moments of joy and excitement, knowing that a new life is growing within.

The Strength to Overcome

Despite the challenges, many teenage mothers rise to the occasion. They continue their education, work tirelessly to provide for their children, and prove that while their journey may have started differently, their love and devotion to their child are no less than that of any other mother.

Many young mothers find support through programs, mentors, and family members who believe in them.

They learn to navigate motherhood while still figuring out their own lives. They develop a level of resilience and determination that sets them apart, knowing that they are not just raising a child—they are proving to themselves and the world that they are capable and strong.

Breaking the Stigma

Society often places a stigma on teenage mothers, labeling them as irresponsible or doomed to failure. But the truth is, many young mothers go on to build successful lives, raise intelligent and compassionate children, and become role models for others in similar situations.

Motherhood at any age is about love, growth, and perseverance. While teenage motherhood presents unique challenges, it also fosters incredible strength, maturity, and an unbreakable bond between mother and child.

Later-in-Life Motherhood – A Different Perspective

Motherhood in the later years of life brings a unique perspective, one shaped by wisdom, patience, and a deep sense of self.

Whether by choice or circumstance, many women are embracing motherhood in their late 30s, 40s, and even 50s, proving that there is no "right" time to become a mother.

The Journey to Late Motherhood

For some women, the decision to wait comes from prioritizing career, travel, or personal growth before settling into motherhood.

Others face fertility struggles that delay their journey, requiring medical interventions like IVF, surrogacy, or adoption. Some women find love later in life and choose to start their families when the timing feels right.

Regardless of the path, later-in-life mothers bring a depth of experience that shapes their parenting style. They often have a greater sense of emotional stability, financial security, and a clear understanding of who they are before stepping into the role of motherhood.

The Advantages and Challenges

One of the greatest advantages of later motherhood is patience. Women who become mothers later in life often feel more confident in their parenting abilities and less influenced by societal pressures or opinions.

They have spent years building their careers, developing life skills, and understanding what truly matters.

However, later motherhood also comes with its own set of challenges. Pregnancy at an older age can carry increased health risks, including complications like gestational diabetes or high blood pressure.

The energy required to keep up with a toddler in their 40s or 50s can be exhausting, and there may be concerns about being an older parent as their child grows.

Despite these challenges, many later-in-life mothers express immense gratitude for the opportunity to experience motherhood on their terms.

Their journey may have been longer, but the love they give is just as deep, and the lessons they pass down are rich with wisdom.

Motherhood Without Age Limits

The idea that motherhood must happen within a certain timeframe is outdated. Women are proving that love, care, and devotion to a child are not dictated by age.

Whether becoming a mother at 18 or 45, the essence of motherhood remains the same; nurturing, protecting, and loving a child unconditionally.

The Choice to Become a Mother – Adoption, IVF, and Unexpected Journeys

Not all paths to motherhood follow the traditional route. Some women find themselves longing for children but unable to conceive naturally.

Others feel called to adopt, providing a loving home to a child in need. Some face unexpected detours, discovering that the journey to motherhood is filled with twists, turns, and moments of uncertainty.

The Struggles of Infertility

For many women, infertility is a heartbreaking reality. The longing to conceive, the countless doctor visits, the failed treatments, and the emotional toll of trying to become a mother can be overwhelming. Yet, many women who walk this path find themselves stronger than they ever imagined.

Advancements in medicine have made options like IVF, surrogacy, and egg donation more accessible.

While these processes can be expensive and emotionally draining, they offer hope to women who dream of holding their own child in their arms.

The Beauty of Adoption

Adoption is another beautiful and valid path to motherhood. Some women choose to adopt after struggling with infertility, while others feel a deep calling to provide a loving home to a child in need.

The process can be long and complex, but the love shared between an adoptive mother and child is just as powerful as any biological bond.

Embracing the Unexpected

Motherhood does not always arrive in the way we expect. Some women find themselves raising stepchildren as their own, blending families with love and patience.

Others take on the role of mother for younger siblings or relatives, stepping in where they are needed most.

Regardless of the path, motherhood is not defined by biology alone; it is defined by love, sacrifice, and the willingness to nurture a child with an open heart.

Refection Thoughts

The journey to motherhood is as diverse as the women who walk it. Whether young or older, biological or adoptive, single or partnered, every mother's story is unique.

What unites them all is the unwavering love they have for their children and the resilience it takes to embrace the role of motherhood, no matter how they arrived there.

In the next chapter, we will explore the art of raising children; how to nurture, guide, and prepare them for the world while balancing the endless demands of being a mother.

Teenage Motherhood – Challenges and Triumphs

I am stronger than my circumstances, and I embrace my journey with courage and love.

My age does not define my ability to be a loving and capable mother.

Every challenge I overcome makes me a more resilient and empowered mother.

Later-in-Life Motherhood – A Different Perspective

I trust that my timing is perfect, and I embrace motherhood with wisdom and grace.

I am equipped with patience, experience, and love to nurture my child in the best way possible.

Motherhood is not defined by age but by the depth of love I give and receive.

The Choice to Become a Mother – Adoption, IVF, and Unexpected Journeys

The path to motherhood may be different, but my love is just as deep and meaningful.

I trust the journey, knowing that I am meant to be a mother in the way that is right for me.

Love, not biology, is what truly makes a mother, and my love is boundless and unconditional.

Chapter 2: The Art of Raising Children

Raising a child is one of life's greatest responsibilities and privileges.

It requires patience, love, wisdom, and adaptability. Each child is unique, with their own needs, personality, and challenges, making parenting a continuous learning experience.

This chapter explores the many aspects of raising children, from nurturing them in their early years to guiding them through adolescence and eventually preparing them for adulthood.

Parenthood is not about perfection; it is about presence, love, and the ability to shape a child's life with care, understanding, and unwavering support.

Building a Strong Foundation – Love, Security, and Discipline

A child's early years are crucial in shaping who they become. The foundation of love, security, and discipline that parents establish during these formative years influences a child's confidence, emotional well-being, and ability to navigate the world.

The Power of Unconditional Love

Children thrive when they feel loved, accepted, and valued. Unconditional love does not mean spoiling or giving in to every demand; rather, it means consistently showing up, reassuring them that they are worthy, and loving them through their successes and failures alike.

Love is expressed through actions; hugging them, listening without judgment, and spending quality time together.

It is the small, everyday moments that build a child's self-esteem and create a deep parent-child bond that lasts a lifetime.

Creating a Sense of Security

A child's first sense of safety comes from their home and caregivers. Security is not just about physical protection; it is also emotional and mental stability.

Children need to know they have a safe place to return to, where they are valued, and where their emotions are acknowledged and respected.

Consistency, routines, and predictability help children feel secure. Knowing what to expect creates a sense of stability, whether through bedtime rituals, family meals, or daily affirmations.

Balancing Love with Discipline

Discipline is often misunderstood as punishment, but true discipline is about guidance and teaching.

Children need boundaries to feel safe, and they thrive when they understand expectations and consequences.

Discipline should be fair, consistent, and based on respect. Rather than focusing solely on correcting bad behavior, discipline should teach children how to make better choices.

Leading by example is one of the most powerful ways to instill good values and habits in a child.

Affirmations for Building a Strong Foundation:

I provide my child with love, security, and guidance to help them grow into their best self.

My discipline is rooted in love and teaches my child valuable life lessons.

I am creating a home filled with warmth, trust, and understanding.

Guiding Children Through Different Stages of Growth

Children go through various stages of growth, and each phase presents new challenges and opportunities for learning. Understanding these stages allows parents to guide their children with patience and wisdom.

Early Childhood – Curiosity and Learning

The early years are filled with curiosity, exploration, and rapid development. Young children learn through play, observation, and imitation. They begin forming their sense of identity and understanding their world.

At this stage, parents should nurture a child's curiosity by encouraging questions, creativity, and exploration. Reading together, playing, and allowing them to express themselves freely are keyways to support their development.

Adolescence – Independence and Identity

Teenage years bring new struggles and joys. Adolescents seek independence while still needing guidance. They begin to form their own identities, challenge authority, and explore different perspectives.

Parents must shift their approach from control to mentorship. Listening without immediate judgment, encouraging open communication, and setting clear yet flexible boundaries help teenagers navigate this stage successfully.

Young Adulthood – Preparing for the World

As children transition into adulthood, they must learn responsibility, resilience, and decision-making. Parents can support this transition by teaching financial literacy, emotional intelligence, and life skills.

Rather than solving every problem for them, parents should equip their children with the tools to handle challenges independently. Encouraging critical thinking, allowing them to make mistakes, and being a source of support rather than control helps them become confident adults.

Affirmations for Guiding Children Through Growth:

I embrace each stage of my child's growth with love, patience, and understanding.

I guide my child with wisdom, teaching them independence while being their support system.

I trust that I am preparing my child to navigate the world with confidence and strength.

Teaching Values, Respect, and Emotional Intelligence

Raising a child is not just about meeting their physical needs; it is about shaping their character, morals, and emotional well-being. Teaching values, respect, and emotional intelligence gives children the tools to build healthy relationships and make wise choices.

Instilling Core Values

Children learn values through observation. Honesty, kindness, gratitude, and empathy are best taught through example. When parents model integrity, generosity, and respect, children internalize these values and carry them into adulthood.

Teaching children to appreciate the value of hard work, accountability, and compassion builds their sense of responsibility and social awareness.

Encouraging acts of kindness, volunteering, and showing gratitude are powerful ways to reinforce positive values.

Teaching Respect for Themselves and Others

Respect starts at home. When children are treated with respect, they learn to extend the same courtesy to others.

This includes teaching them to respect personal boundaries, opinions, and differences.

Teaching children to speak kindly, listen actively, and resolve conflicts peacefully helps them build strong, meaningful relationships.

It also helps them develop confidence and self-respect.

Developing Emotional Intelligence

Emotional intelligence—the ability to recognize, understand, and manage emotions—is a critical life skill. Children who develop emotional intelligence have better self-control, empathy, and resilience.

Parents can nurture emotional intelligence by:

Encouraging children to express their emotions in a healthy way.

Teaching them to recognize and manage stress.

Helping them develop problem-solving skills.

By creating a space where children feel safe to talk about their feelings without fear of judgment, parents empower them to handle life's ups and downs with grace and confidence.

Affirmations for Teaching Values, Respect, and Emotional Intelligence:

I am raising a child who is kind, respectful, and emotionally strong.

I lead by example, teaching my child the importance of honesty, compassion, and gratitude.

I encourage my child to express their emotions and navigate challenges with wisdom and confidence.

Reflection Thoughts

Parenting is an evolving journey filled with lessons, triumphs, and moments of uncertainty. No two children are the same, and there is no single "right" way to raise them.

However, love, consistency, and patience form the foundation of successful parenting.

As parents, we are not just raising children, we are raising future adults, leaders, and members of society.

By nurturing them with love, guiding them with wisdom, and teaching them to respect themselves and others, we equip them to navigate life with confidence and purpose.

In the next chapter, we will explore the realities of single parenting—how to balance responsibilities, overcome challenges, and create a nurturing environment despite doing it alone.

Chapter 3: Single Motherhood – Strength in the Journey

Single motherhood is a path that requires resilience, determination, and an abundance of love. Whether by choice, circumstance, or unforeseen life events, raising a child alone presents unique challenges and profound rewards.

This chapter explores the reality of single parenting—the struggles, sacrifices, and triumphs. It highlights the strength of single mothers who carry the weight of responsibility while still nurturing, guiding, and uplifting their children.

Despite the difficulties, single motherhood is not a journey of loneliness; it is a journey of strength, self-discovery, and unwavering love.

The Challenges and Triumphs of Single Motherhood

Single motherhood is a balancing act—juggling work, finances, parenting, and personal well-being. Many single mothers face financial struggles, emotional exhaustion, and societal judgment. However, they also develop incredible inner strength, independence, and resilience.

Financial Struggles and Stability

One of the most common challenges single mothers face is financial hardship. Raising a child on one income often requires careful budgeting, sacrifices, and strategic planning. Many single mothers work multiple jobs, return to school, or start side businesses to ensure their children have everything they need.

While financial stress can be overwhelming, it also pushes single mothers to become resourceful. They find creative ways to stretch their budget, seek community resources, and teach their children financial responsibility.

Emotional Strength and Mental Well-being

Raising a child alone can be emotionally exhausting. The weight of making every decision, the constant worry, and the pressure to be both mother and father can lead to burnout. Single mothers often struggle with self-doubt and the fear of not doing "enough" for their children.

Yet, despite the emotional toll, single mothers develop an unmatched inner strength. They learn to lean on their own resilience, prioritize self-care, and build support systems to navigate the challenges.

The Triumph of Independence and Strength

Though single motherhood is difficult, it is also empowering. Many women discover a strength they never knew they had.

They learn to trust themselves, embrace their independence, and find joy in the small victories—whether it's celebrating a child's success, overcoming a tough financial situation, or simply making it through a challenging day.

Affirmations for The Challenges and Triumphs of Single Motherhood:

I am capable, strong, and resourceful.

I can handle any challenge that comes my way.

I am enough for my child, providing them with love, security, and guidance.

Each struggle I overcome makes me a stronger, wiser, and more resilient mother.

Creating a Support System and Finding Balance

No single mother should have to navigate this journey alone. Building a strong support system and finding balance is essential for both the mother's well-being and the child's development.

The Importance of a Support System

A strong support system provides emotional, financial, and practical assistance. Whether it's family, close friends, or community resources, having people to lean on can make all the difference.

Single mothers often turn to their own parents, siblings, or close friends for help with childcare, financial emergencies, or simply emotional support.

Some find comfort in joining single-parent support groups, seeking professional counseling, or participating in faith-based communities.

Asking for help is not a sign of weakness—it is a sign of strength and wisdom. No one is meant to do everything alone, and having a network of support can lighten the load.

Balancing Parenting, Work, and Personal Life

Many single mothers struggle with balancing work and parenting. The demands of a job, household responsibilities, and raising children often leave little time for personal well-being. However, balance is possible with intentional effort:

Prioritization – Focusing on what truly matters and letting go of unnecessary stress.

Time Management – Establishing routines and schedules to create stability for both the mother and child.

Self-Care – Taking moments for personal health, hobbies, and rest, even if it's just a few minutes each day.

Finding balance does not mean having a "perfect" life—it means creating a life where both mother and child can thrive.

Teaching Children the Value of Independence and Responsibility

Single mothers often raise highly independent and responsible children. When children see their mother working hard and managing responsibilities alone, they learn resilience, problem-solving, and gratitude.

By encouraging children to contribute to household tasks, make responsible choices, and develop self-sufficiency, single mothers prepare them for adulthood in a way that strengthens their character and life skills.

Affirmations for Creating a Support System and Finding Balance:

I am not alone—support and love surround me in many forms.

I create balance in my life by prioritizing what truly matters.

I am raising a strong, independent child who values responsibility and love.

Embracing the Journey – Strength, Love, and Self-Worth

Single motherhood is more than just a role; it is a powerful journey of self-discovery, resilience, and love. Every challenge faced and overcome adds to a mother's strength.

Letting Go of Guilt and Embracing Self-Love

Many single mothers experience guilt; guilt for working long hours, guilt for not providing a two-parent household, or guilt for not always having enough time. However, guilt serves no purpose other than to drain emotional energy.

Instead of dwelling on guilt, single mothers should embrace self-love and acknowledge their efforts. Every single day, they show up for their children, give their best, and create a life filled with love and lessons. That is more than enough.

Celebrating Every Victory—Big or Small

Small victories matter. Whether it's a child reaching a milestone, overcoming a tough day, or simply keeping the household running, every success should be celebrated.

Single mothers often do not give themselves enough credit, but they should. They are warriors, shaping their children's futures with love, patience, and perseverance.

Recognizing Self-Worth and the Beauty of the Journey

Single motherhood is not about struggle, it is about strength. It is about discovering that even in the hardest moments, there is joy. It is about knowing that love is what makes a family, not circumstances.

A single mother is not defined by her challenges but by her ability to rise above them. She is worthy, powerful, and capable of creating a beautiful life for both herself and her child.

Affirmations for Embracing the Journey – Strength, Love, and Self-Worth:

I release guilt and embrace the love and strength I bring to my child's life.

Every small victory is worth celebrating—I am doing an amazing job as a mother.

I am powerful, worthy, and capable of creating a joyful and fulfilling life.

Reflection Thoughts

Single motherhood is a journey of love, strength, and transformation. While the path may be challenging, it is also deeply rewarding. Single mothers are proof that love and resilience can overcome any obstacle.

By embracing support, creating balance, and recognizing their worth, single mothers not only raise strong children but also become the strongest versions of themselves.

In the next chapter, we will explore the challenges and triumphs of raising adult children who still live at home; how to set boundaries, encourage independence, and maintain a healthy parent-child relationship.

Chapter 4: When They Never Leave – Adult Children at Home

The image of a child leaving home to build their own life has long been a milestone of adulthood. But in today's world, more and more adult children are staying home longer; or even returning after trying to make it on their own.

While having an adult child at home can be a source of comfort, it can also bring unexpected challenges, such as financial strain, lack of privacy, and struggles with independence.

This chapter explores why adult children stay home, how parents can set healthy boundaries, and ways to encourage independence while maintaining a strong parent-child relationship.

The Changing Landscape of Adulthood

In the past, it was expected that young adults would leave home by their early twenties, either for college, marriage, or work.

However, today's economic realities, shifting cultural norms, and changing family dynamics have made this transition less predictable.

Why Are Adult Children Staying Home Longer?

Several factors contribute to the growing trend of adult children living at home:

Financial Hardships – The rising cost of living, student loan debt, and job instability make it difficult for young adults to afford rent and other expenses.

Delayed Marriage and Family Planning – Many young adults are postponing marriage and parenthood, leading to fewer pressures to establish their own households.

Mental Health and Emotional Factors – Some young adults struggle with anxiety, depression, or a lack of confidence, making it harder for them to take the next step toward independence.

Cultural and Family Expectations – In some cultures, multigenerational living is normal and expected, while in others, it is becoming a necessity due to economic conditions.

Navigating the Shift in Parenting Dynamics

The parent-child relationship evolves when a child becomes an adult, but when they remain in the home, this shift can be unclear.

Parents may feel they are still in a caregiving role, while the adult child may struggle with asserting independence.

Finding a new balance is key, one that honors the child's adulthood while maintaining mutual respect and household harmony.

Affirmations for The Changing Landscape of Adulthood:

I embrace this new phase of parenthood with patience and understanding.

My home is a place of love and support, but also of growth and responsibility.

I can guide my adult child while respecting their independence.

Setting Boundaries and Expectations

One of the biggest challenges of having an adult child at home is maintaining a healthy balance between support and independence. Without clear expectations, frustration can build on both sides.

Establishing Household Rules and Responsibilities

Just because an adult child is living at home does not mean they are exempt from contributing to the household. It's important to have a conversation about responsibilities, including:

Financial Contributions – Should they pay rent or help with groceries and utilities?

Chores and Household Duties – Who is responsible for cleaning, cooking, and maintaining shared spaces?

Personal Freedom vs. Household **Consideration** – How do late nights, guests, and personal habits impact the rest of the household?

By discussing these topics openly, parents can avoid resentment and create a living arrangement that works for everyone.

Encouraging Independence Without Forcing It

While it's tempting to push an adult child toward independence, they need to feel ready. Instead of making them feel unwelcome, parents can take steps to empower them, such as:

Helping them create a plan for moving out.

Encouraging job or career growth.

Supporting financial literacy and budgeting skills.

This allows them to take ownership of their future while feeling supported, not pressured.

Affirmations for Setting Boundaries and Expectations:

I set boundaries that promote harmony and personal growth in my home.

I encourage my adult child to take steps toward independence with love and support.

Healthy boundaries strengthen relationships and teach responsibility.

Preparing for the Next Chapter – Letting Go and Moving Forward

At some point, the goal is for adult children to leave home and establish their own lives. While this transition can be difficult for both parent and child, it is a natural and necessary step.

Helping Adult Children Transition to Independence

If an adult child is hesitant to move out, parents can offer guidance in ways that make the process feel more manageable:

Creating a Timeline – Setting a reasonable move-out date can help both parent and child prepare for the change.

Financial Planning – Teaching budgeting, savings, and money management ensures they are financially ready.

Emotional Support – Reassuring them that independence does not mean losing family support.

Letting Go Without Guilt

Parents may feel a mix of emotions when their adult child leaves home; pride, relief, sadness, or even loneliness. Some worry whether they have done enough to prepare them for the real world.

Letting go does not mean stopping love and support; it means trusting that the foundation has been laid, and now it is time for them to step into their own life.

Embracing a New Phase of Life

Once the child moves out, parents can embrace new opportunities:

Reconnecting with personal goals and hobbies.

Strengthening relationships with a spouse, friends, or community.

Enjoying newfound freedom and space.

This transition is not an end, but a beginning, a chance for both parent and child to grow into the next stage of their lives.

Affirmations for Preparing for the Next Chapter:

I trust that my child is ready for the next step in their journey.

I release fear and embrace the joy of new beginnings—for both of us.

Letting go is an act of love, not loss.

Reflection Thoughts

Having an adult child at home can be both a blessing and a challenge. While offering support is important, so is encouraging independence.

By setting clear boundaries, fostering growth, and preparing for the future, parents can create a healthy transition for both themselves and their children.

In the next chapter, we will explore the resilience, empowerment, and courage that mothers develop through all stages of parenthood, celebrating the strength that defines a mother's love.

Chapter 5: The Evolution of a Mother's Role

Motherhood is a journey of continuous transformation. From the moment a woman becomes a mother, she embarks on a lifelong evolution; adapting to new phases, challenges, and responsibilities.

What begins as nurturing an infant shifts into guiding a child, supporting a teenager, and eventually letting go as they step into adulthood.

This chapter explores the changing roles of a mother through different stages of life, the emotional adjustments required, and the strength, wisdom, and resilience that develop along the way.

From Caregiver to Guide – The Shifting Responsibilities

In the early years, a mother is the primary caregiver—feeding, soothing, and protecting her child. Her role is centered on meeting every need, ensuring safety, and providing comfort. However, as a child grows, the responsibilities of motherhood change, shifting from direct care to guidance and support.

The Different Stages of Motherhood

Infancy & Early Childhood (The Nurturer)

Providing love, protection, and basic needs.

Teaching first lessons about love and security.

Experiencing the overwhelming responsibility of shaping a new life.

School Years (The Teacher & Protector)

Helping children navigate friendships, school, and emotions.

Establishing discipline and structure while encouraging independence.

Balancing being a loving parent and an authority figure.

Teen Years (The Advisor & Boundary-Setter)

Navigating the emotional rollercoaster of adolescence.

Letting go of control while offering guidance.

Learning to communicate differently, as the child seeks independence.

Adulthood (The Supporter & Friend)

Encouraging without overstepping.

Respecting their choices while still offering wisdom.

Shifting from parenting to companionship and emotional support.

This transition is not always easy. Many mothers struggle with the changing dynamics, unsure of how to let go while remaining connected.

However, embracing these shifts allows for growth in both the mother and child.

Affirmations for The Shifting Responsibilities:

I accept and embrace the changing seasons of motherhood with grace.

I guide my child with wisdom, trusting in the lessons I have taught.

I am always a mother, but my role evolves as my child grows.

Balancing Self-Identity and Motherhood

Many women find that becoming a mother reshapes their sense of self. The early years of parenting are often consumed by meeting the needs of others, and it's easy to lose sight of personal goals and dreams.

However, as children grow more independent, mothers have the opportunity to rediscover their own identity beyond their role as a parent.

Reclaiming Personal Passions

Revisiting hobbies and interests that may have been set aside.

Exploring new career paths or educational goals.

Finding joy in self-care, travel, or creative expression.

The Guilt of Prioritizing Oneself

Many mothers struggle with guilt when they begin to focus on themselves. Society often praises self-sacrifice, making women feel that personal fulfillment should come second to family needs.

However, embracing personal growth sets a powerful example for children; showing them the importance of balance and self-love.

Creating a Life Beyond Motherhood

While motherhood is a defining role, it is not the only role a woman plays.

Cultivating friendships, pursuing personal ambitions, and maintaining a sense of self enriches both the mother and the family dynamic.

A fulfilled woman creates a happier and healthier household.

Affirmations for Balancing Self-Identity and Motherhood:

I am a mother, but I am also a woman with dreams and passions.

Prioritizing my own growth makes me a stronger and happier mother.

I embrace all parts of myself—mother, individual, and dreamer.

The Legacy of a Mother's Love

As children grow and build their own lives, a mother's influence does not fade; it simply transforms. The love, lessons, and values she has instilled become part of the next generation.

What We Pass Down to Our Children

Values & Morals – Teaching kindness, resilience, and integrity.

Strength & Perseverance – Demonstrating courage through life's challenges.

Unconditional Love – Ensuring children know they are always supported, no matter where life takes them.

Motherhood's Ripple Effect

A mother's impact extends far beyond her own children. Her wisdom is passed down through generations, influencing how her children parent, how they build relationships, and how they navigate life's challenges.

Embracing the Next Chapter

Many mothers struggle with the "empty nest" phase, feeling a loss of purpose once their children leave home. However, this stage offers a new beginning, one filled with opportunities to focus on personal goals, deepen other relationships, and embrace new adventures.

Letting go does not mean the end of motherhood. It means stepping into a new role; one of mentor, cheerleader, and lifelong supporter.

Affirmations for The Legacy of a Mother's Love:

The love I have given will continue to shape my children's lives forever.

I trust that my guidance has prepared my children for their journey.

Motherhood is eternal, and my influence lives on through love and wisdom.

Reflection Thoughts

Motherhood is not a static role; it is a lifelong journey of change, adaptation, and growth.

From the first moments of holding a newborn to the pride of watching an adult child build their own life, a mother's love remains constant.

Though the responsibilities shift, the bond never fades.

Embracing the evolution of motherhood allows women to grow alongside their children, celebrating each new phase with strength, grace, and love.

In the next chapter, we will explore the importance of gratitude in the motherhood journey; giving thanks for the struggles, the joys, and the countless moments that define a mother's love.

Chapter 6: A Mother's Heart – Gratitude and Reflection

Motherhood is a journey filled with love, challenges, sacrifice, and joy. Through every stage, from pregnancy to raising children and eventually letting them go, mothers experience an evolution of emotions, growth, and self-discovery.

This chapter is dedicated to gratitude, reflecting on the joys and hardships of motherhood, appreciating the lessons learned, and embracing the beauty of a mother's heart. No matter how difficult the path, there is always something to be grateful for.

Gratitude for the Journey – Embracing Every Moment

One of the greatest gifts a mother can give herself is the ability to be present and cherish each stage of the journey.

There are moments of exhaustion, frustration, and even heartbreak, but within those challenges lie profound moments of joy, love, and deep connection.

Finding Gratitude in Every Stage

The Newborn Stage – Sleepless nights, endless diaper changes, and feeding struggles can feel overwhelming.

But in the quiet moments of holding a sleeping baby, feeling their tiny fingers grasp yours, or hearing their first coo, gratitude emerges. The exhaustion fades, but the love remains.

The Toddler & Childhood Years – The days are long, filled with tantrums, endless questions, and boundless energy.

Yet, this is the stage where children express pure love; running into your arms, drawing pictures just for you, and looking at you as their entire world. These are the moments to cherish.

The Teenage Years – Independence begins to form, and sometimes it feels like children pull away.

There may be arguments, misunderstandings, and the pain of not being their first choice anymore.

But there is gratitude in watching them grow into themselves, making their own choices, and becoming strong, capable individuals.

Adulthood & Letting Go – When children leave home, there is an aching emptiness.

But there is also gratitude; gratitude for the privilege of raising them, for the love shared, and for knowing that they carry a piece of their mother's heart wherever they go.

Practicing Daily Gratitude as a Mother

Take a moment each day to reflect on something positive in your motherhood journey.

Keep a gratitude journal, jotting down small moments that bring joy.

Express gratitude to your children, letting them know how much they are loved and appreciated.

Affirmations for Gratitude in Motherhood:

I embrace every stage of motherhood with love and gratitude.

Even in difficult moments, I find joy in the journey of being a mother.

The love I give and receive as a mother is my greatest blessing.

Learning from the Challenges – Growth Through Struggles

Motherhood is not without its difficulties. There are times when exhaustion, worry, and feelings of failure can weigh heavily.

But within those challenges lies growth, resilience, and a deepened sense of love.

The Strength Found in Hardship

Financial Struggles – Many mothers experience the burden of making ends meet.

Providing for a child can be stressful, but it also teaches resourcefulness, determination, and gratitude for the little things.

Single Motherhood – Raising children alone can feel isolating and overwhelming. But through it, mothers discover their own strength, independence, and an unbreakable bond with their children.

Letting Go of Control – As children grow, they make their own choices, some good, some painful to watch.

The challenge is in letting them learn from their own mistakes while continuing to be a source of guidance and love.

Every hardship carries a lesson. Every challenge strengthens a mother's heart.

Finding Gratitude in the Hard Times

Instead of focusing on struggles, reflect on what they have taught you.

Recognize that through the hardest days, you have become stronger, wiser, and more compassionate.

Give yourself grace; no mother is perfect, but every mother loves perfectly in her own way.

Affirmations for Growth Through Challenges:

I am grateful for the lessons that motherhood has taught me.

Every challenge I face makes me stronger and more resilient.

I give myself grace, knowing that I am doing my best as a mother.

Leaving a Legacy – A Mother's Love Lives On

Long after children have grown and built their own lives, a mother's love remains.

The lessons taught, the sacrifices made, and the unconditional love given create a legacy that lasts for generations.

What We Leave Behind

Memories of Love – The bedtime stories, the warm hugs, the whispered "I love you's" will always stay with our children.

Lessons in Strength & Kindness – How we handle adversity, treat others, and navigate life will influence how our children live their own lives.

Unbreakable Bonds – Even if miles separate a mother and child, love knows no distance.

Embracing the Next Chapter

As children grow, a mother's role shifts. Instead of focusing on raising them, the focus turns to supporting them in their own journey.

This is a time for mothers to rediscover themselves; to pursue passions, embrace new adventures, and cherish the relationships they have built.

Motherhood never truly ends; it simply evolves. A mother's heart beats in every lesson taught, every sacrifice made, and every ounce of love given.

Affirmations for Leaving a Legacy:

My love and wisdom will live on in my children and future generations.

I am proud of the mother I have been and continue to be.

Motherhood is eternal, and my heart is full of love and gratitude.

Final Reflection

Motherhood is an ever-changing, ever-evolving journey filled with love, learning, and immense gratitude.

Each stage—whether filled with joy or difficulty; shapes the woman who embarks on this incredible path.

As we close this book, take a moment to reflect on your own journey. What are you most grateful for?

What lessons have you learned?

What legacy do you hope to leave behind?

Above all, know this: A mother's heart is one of the most powerful forces in the world. It is filled with love, resilience, and endless gratitude. And that love will never fade.

Why I Wrote This Book

I wrote this book because motherhood is not a one-size-fits-all experience. Each journey is unique, yet so many of us share similar joys, fears, and triumphs.

I have seen teenage mothers rise above adversity, single mothers carry the weight of the world with grace, and older mothers embrace the beauty of parenthood later in life.

I have witnessed the struggles of raising children, the heartbreak of letting them go, and the reality of welcoming them back home as adults.

Motherhood is a lifelong commitment, one that changes with time but never truly ends. The role of a mother evolves, but the love remains constant.

This book is a celebration of that love and a reflection of the strength it takes to be a mother in all its forms. Whether you are a new mother, an experienced one, or someone preparing for the journey ahead, I hope these pages inspire you, validate your experiences, and remind you that you are never alone in this journey.

Because motherhood is more than a role, it is a legacy of love, resilience, and the ability to shape the future, one child at a time.

Helpful Resources

No matter where you are in your journey, expecting your first child, raising teenagers, parenting solo, or adjusting to an empty (or still-full) nest—know that help, support, and community are within reach. Below are some carefully chosen resources to encourage, uplift, and support you.

Parenting & Single Motherhood Support

Single Mothers by Choice – www.singlemothersbychoice.org

A supportive network of women who are thinking about or have chosen to raise children on their own.

Parents Without Partners – www.parentswithoutpartners.org

A community for single parents to connect, share, and learn from one another.

National Parent Helpline – [1-855-4A-PARENT (1-855-427-2736)]

Emotional support and guidance from trained advocates for any parent feeling overwhelmed.

Books on Motherhood, Growth, and Resilience

Operating Instructions by Anne Lamott – A raw, humorous, and honest memoir of single motherhood.

The Gifts of Imperfect Parenting by Brené Brown – A guide to raising wholehearted children and embracing imperfect parenting.

The Conscious Parent by Dr. Shefali Tsabary – Offers transformative insights into parenting through self-awareness.

Self-Care & Emotional Well-being

Calm App – www.calm.com

Meditation, sleep, and relaxation tools tailored to busy parents and overwhelmed hearts.

Therapy for Black Girls –
www.therapyforblackgirls.com

A mental health platform supporting Black women and mothers through licensed therapists and resources.

Postpartum Support International –
www.postpartum.net

Help for mothers facing postpartum depression, anxiety, or emotional challenges after birth.

Support for Mothers of Adult Children

Mothers of Adult Children Support Group (on Facebook)

A private, judgment-free space to share and receive support from mothers of grown children.

"Done With The Crying" by Sheri McGregor

A powerful resource for parents navigating estrangement or the complexities of adult children still living at home.

Spiritual & Faith-Based Encouragement

Proverbs 31 Ministries –

www.proverbs31.org

Daily devotionals, prayer support, and encouragement for women of faith.

Faithful Counseling –

www.faithfulcounseling.com

Online therapy from a Christian perspective.

Remember:

You are not alone. You are doing sacred work.

Reach out. Refill your cup. Reclaim your peace.

About the Author

As I close the final pages of this book, I do so not just as an author, but as a woman who has lived the many roles and realities of motherhood.

I am a sister, shaped by shared memories, secrets, and a bond that only siblings understand.

I am a wife, having known both the comfort and complexity of partnership.

I am a mother, who has carried the weight of tiny hearts and grown into the role with love, mistakes, sacrifice, and fierce protection.

I am a grandmother and great-grandmother—graced with the rare and beautiful privilege of watching love bloom through generations.

My journey, like many of yours, has been far from perfect. There were seasons when outside influences, family expectations, friends' opinions, cultural obligations—tried to define who I should be as a woman and a mother.

I carried responsibilities that weren't mine alone and often poured from an empty cup.

There were moments of quiet loneliness. Times when, surrounded by everyone, I still felt unseen. Moments I gave until there was nothing left but silence and a tired heart.

That is the truth of motherhood that no one talks about: the invisible weight we bear, and the strength it takes to carry it with grace.

But through it all, I remained. I rose. I loved. I endured.

This book is a reflection of all those versions of me—and maybe, all the versions of you, too. It's a thank-you to the woman I was, a love letter to the woman I've become, and a hopeful embrace to every woman walking this path now.

We may carry different stories, but we share the same strength.

We may walk different paths, but we hold the same light in our hearts.

I hope this book makes you feel seen.

I hope it reminds you that you are not alone.

And above all, I hope it affirms what you already know in your soul:

You are a mother and that, in itself, is everything.

With heartfelt gratitude, Vgdawson

Stay Connected

Thank you for sharing this journey with me.

If this book touched your heart, made you feel seen, or reminded you of your own strength, I'd love to hear from you.

Let's keep the conversation going:

Follow my author journey:

Website: www.what2buynext.com

Instagram: @what2buynexy

Facebook: what2buynext - Author

For speaking engagements, book clubs, or personal messages:

Email: support@what2buynext.com

Explore my full book collection and products:

Visit my shop for books, affirmations, candles, and more:

www.what2buynext.com/articles

You are not alone. You are not invisible. You are enough.

Let's keep growing, healing, and honoring the sacred work of motherhood—together.

Stop Regretting the Past and
Start Designing a Life You
Love

Vgdawson

So many women spend years
apologizing for the past,
replaying old wounds, and
carrying regret for choices
they made when they didn't
know better. But here is the
truth: your past is not a life sentence.

WHAT YOU
DON'T
CHANGE,
YOU
CHOOSE

*Stop Regretting the Past
and Start Designing a Life You Love*

by vgdawson

What You Don't Change, You Choose is a powerful,
heart-centered guide for women who have
survived, sacrificed, stayed too long, and are finally
ready to stop living in regret and start living on
purpose.

With honesty, compassion, and lived wisdom,
author vgdawson walks you through the defining
moments, wasted years, and silent choices that
shaped your life—then shows you how to reclaim
your power and choose differently.

Author of books on relationships, personal growth,
and life transitions.

The Journey Through
Womanhood

Vgdawson

With honesty and grace,
Becoming Her examines
the emotional weight
women bear while living
for others — family, love,

children, and responsibility — and the awakening
that comes when a woman finally asks, "Who am I
now?"

Through heartfelt storytelling and real-life
reflections, this book speaks to:
Women navigating identity, love, and loss.
Mothers and single parents carrying unseen
burdens.
Women healing from disappointment, regret, or
unmet expectations.
Anyone ready to rediscover themselves after years
of giving.
This is not a book of judgment — it is a book of
understanding.
Not a guide to perfection — but an invitation to
growth, forgiveness, and renewal.

Author of books on relationships, personal growth,
and life transitions.

Dear Self: A Letter to the Self Who Endured

Reflections and Resilience Across Life's Journey
Reflections 40/50/60

Vgdawson

What if the life you lived— every choice, every heartbreak, every quiet victory—was preparing you to finally come home to yourself?

Dear Self: Reflections and Resilience Across Life's Journey is a heartfelt letter written after years of living, learning, and surviving what no one talks about. It's for the woman who reached her 30s, 40s, or 50s and began asking the hard questions—*Why didn't life turn out the way I planned? Why did I love so deeply and still feel unseen? Why am I still standing after everything I've endured?*

Author of books on relationships, personal growth, and life transitions.

The Journey of Motherhood

"In the quiet moments, when no one sees and no one hears, a mother's love still speaks. It is in those sacred, unseen acts of sacrifice and strength that our legacy is born. I may not have done it perfectly, but I did it with all the love I had—and that was always enough."

— Vgdawson

Thank You

To every reader who picked up this book—thank you.

Thank you for opening your heart to my words, for walking with me through the layers of motherhood, and for honoring the deep, complex, beautiful journey we all share.

To the mothers who saw themselves in these pages: your strength is real, your sacrifices are seen, and your love—though often unspoken—is felt across generations.

To the women doing it all alone, to those surrounded by support, and to those somewhere in between—thank you for showing up every day, even when the world doesn't notice.

To my daughters, daughters-in-law, granddaughters, and every woman raising children with courage and grace: thank you for continuing the story. I am proud of you. I believe in you. And I am always here cheering you on.

And lastly, thank you to my own heart—for surviving, for enduring, and for continuing to love, even in loneliness. This book is as much a gift to others as it is a healing for myself.

With love and gratitude,

Vgdawson

The Journey of Motherhood

Strength, Love & Resilience

www.ingramcontent.com/pod-product-compliance
Lightning Source LLC
Chambersburg PA
CBHW051414050726
47595CB00010B/4059